To:

_____

From:

_____

Our Love is never ending...

The Handcrafted Letter

The Handcrafted Letter

Diane Maurer-Mathison

Photographs by Giles D. Prett

STOREY BOOKS

Pownal, Vermont 05261

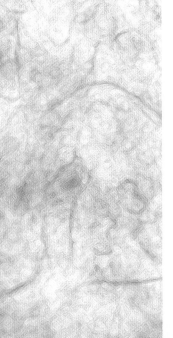

THE MISSION of
Storey Communications
is to serve our customers
by publishing practical
information that
encourages personal
independence in harmony
with the environment.

Edited by Deborah Balmuth and Karen Levy
Cover design by Leslie Constantino
Art direction, text design, and photo styling by Cynthia N. McFarland
Photo styling assistance by Karen Levy
Layout assistance by Erin Lincourt
Calligraphy on pages 21, 25, 26, 47, 70, and 84 by Ann Kremers
Indexed by Ty Koontz

Thanks to The Left Bank Gallery, Bennington, Vermont, for the loan of materials; Stampendous (page 85) and Stamp Francisco (page 80) for the use of their rubber stamps; and Nature's Pressed for the pressed flowers used throughout the book.

Copyright © 2001 by Diane Maurer-Mathison

The information in this book is true and complete to the best of our knowledge. All recommendations are made without guarantee on the part of the author or Storey Books. The author and publisher disclaim any liability in connection with the use of this information. For additional information, please contact Storey Books, Schoolhouse Road, Pownal, Vermont 05261.

Storey Books are available for special premium and promotional uses and for customized editions. For further information, please call Storey's Custom Publishing Department at (800) 793-9396.

Printed in the United Kingdom by Butler & Tanner, Ltd.
10 9 8 7 6 5 4 3 2 1

LIBRARY OF CONGRESS CATALOGING-IN-PUBLICATION DATA

Maurer-Mathison, Diane V., 1944-
    The handcrafted letter : Get inspired, find your voice, & create unique projects to keep in touch / by Diane Maurer-Mathison.
        p. cm.
    ISBN 1-58017-360-8 (alk. paper)
    1. Greeting cards. 2. Paper work. I. Title.

TT872 .M33 2001
745.594'1—dc21
                                            00-067959

Contents

For Jennifer, whose delightful thank-you letters often outshine the gifts.

Sincere thanks to contributing artists

Laura Donnelly Bethmann
(page 20),
Lea Everse *(pages 81, 85),*
Jill Foster, Lynell Harlow
(pages 70, 90),
Mary Anne Landfield
(page 47),
Jennifer Philippoff *(page 97),*
Mary Ryan-Ozburn *(page 81),*
Edie Roberts *(page 72),*
and Jill Taylor
(pages 7, 36, 78, 88).

Rediscovering the Art of Letter Writing

At first, the advent of e-mail seemed like a blessing and a way to quickly connect with friends. You could stay in touch by typing a few sentences and clicking a button to send your words across the miles. There were no envelopes to address, no stamps to affix, *no need to worry* about your handwriting, no possibility of a stain on your paper from a nearby cup of coffee or a blurred letter caused by an affectionate cat nuzzling your pen.

Write to me, even on the tiny sheet though I am obliged to read them as one goes up stairs — two steps forward and one back — not to have done too soon.

Harriet Cavendish
to her sister, 1803

I, too, embraced the technology until I noticed that my calligrapher and artist friends had started e-mailing me instead of sending their beautifully penned and decorated letters and envelopes. Even my oldest friend, Sally, who always sent animated letters with little drawings in the margins and rich descriptions of her days at a wildlife center, reverted to sending short e-mails instead of actual letters.

Letters can discuss something as simple as flowers in bloom.

I not only missed the physical beauty of letters from friends but also longed for the little musings, descriptions, and soul-searching that had fallen by the wayside. The speed with which e-mail could be sent seemed to rush my correspondents. What may have been a long, thoughtful letter laden with memories, dreams, and humorous anecdotes became more like a hurried memo; a poor substitute for real communication.

Thomas Jefferson aptly described the arrival of a letter as being "like the bright beams of the moon on the desolate heath." There is something more intimate about a handwritten letter that e-mails, typed letters, and even phone calls cannot replace. Sending a handwritten letter is like sending a small part of yourself. Your confidant can visit you over and over simply by opening a card or unfolding stationery to see your unique penmanship and feel the honesty and warm embrace of the words you have written.

Handwritten letters not only enrich the lives of the people who receive them, they also benefit those who write them. Using a pen to form words on a page forces us to slow down enough to appreciate and describe the natural world around us, such as the bright blue of the iris blooming beside the pond, the lightning skipping between the clouds, or the sound of the barn owl calling through the wind. Letter writing gives us time to consider our thoughts and feelings and gain insight into our lives as we describe them to others.

In an age of isolation, letter writing makes us feel connected to others and reinforces the fact that our words of encouragement, apology, or empathy can make a difference in their lives. The memories we share with others can rekindle the joys, humor, and excitement of our own lives.

By sharing letters with those who live far away, we can maintain lifelong friendships and establish and nurture intimacy with those whom we rarely see in person. Many of our letters will probably be saved and carefully placed on a scrapbook page, or tied in ribbons and lovingly placed in a special box with the mementos we send. Our great-grandchildren will know us through our handwritten letters and through the letters we save. A letter is more than just a means of communication: It is a gift — and sometimes a legacy.

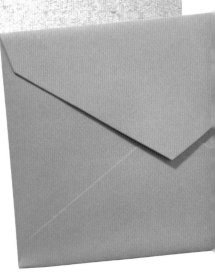

Please dash me off a letter . . . put as many jabs and jibes and sarcasms in it as you have in stock. Blow me a refreshing breeze!

Mark Twain to Mary Rogers, 1906

Writing a Beautiful Letter

Most of us have distinctly personal handwriting that our friends immediately recognize when our letters arrive. Our handwriting is said to *reflect our personality* and our nature. But today it is more likely to reflect the fast pace of our lives and the cluttered state of our desks.

Many people avoid hand writing letters because they are so embarrassed at how illegible their penmanship has become. That, unfortunately, only makes the problem worse; writing deteriorates when we type everything. As we *practice writing slowly* and carefully, we are able to relearn how to make letter forms that flow together quickly and smoothly.

You must improve your penmanship; your writing is like the speaking of a child of three years old — very understandable to its father but to no one else.

John Keats
to a correspondent, 1820

Handwriting **Problems**

Take a good look at something you've written lately, even the grocery list, and chances are you'll find some common errors that can be corrected. You can still maintain your personal style of writing while improving its legibility.

Collapsed Letters

Look for collapsed letters or letters with missing parts: 'e's that look like the letter i, 'a's that look like 'e's, and 't's that are mistaken for 'l's. To correct this, be aware of your writing, slow down, and ease the tension in your hand. Practice by making large letters for a while.

Inconsistent Letterforms

Many people create the same letter in many different ways. We flip-flop our 'r's or 's's and never really decide how we want to form the letter. Decide how you wish to make the letter in question, then force yourself to be consistent.

Slanted Letters

Do your 'l's and 't's look like they are waving to you from the page? Speed writing, an uneven surface, and hand tension can slant letters erratically. Slow down, work on a padded surface, and loosen up by doodling with a pen.

Uphill and Downhill Penmanship

This is a common lefty's problem because of the way the pen is held. Poor posture or writing on a page cocked at a strange angle can also contribute to the problem. Find a better writing area and write on a slanted surface. You can also use a sheet of ruled paper behind thin stationery, or draw a single erasable line at the top of your page and concentrate on writing each line parallel to the one above.

A simple grocery list can indentify
easily correctable handwriting problems.

SIMPLE ITALIC HANDWRITING

A calligraphy course in italic-style writing is a fun gift to give yourself. You can also learn from a book (see Recommended Reading), or begin by just tracing the italic letters shown here. Practicing this style can help you write more beautifully while still maintaining the personality of your own writing. Calligrapher Jill Taylor explains that our handwriting often deteriorates because "in kindergarten we are taught the ball-and-stick method of writing. Then, in grade school, we switch to a slanted cursive with loops and joins. Most of us do not stick with this long enough to master it. By middle school we are doing a mixture of printing and cursive and our writing often becomes illegible."

Begin by practicing the letters without serifs, as shown at right. Later you can add serifs as shown below, which will make natural joins between letters.

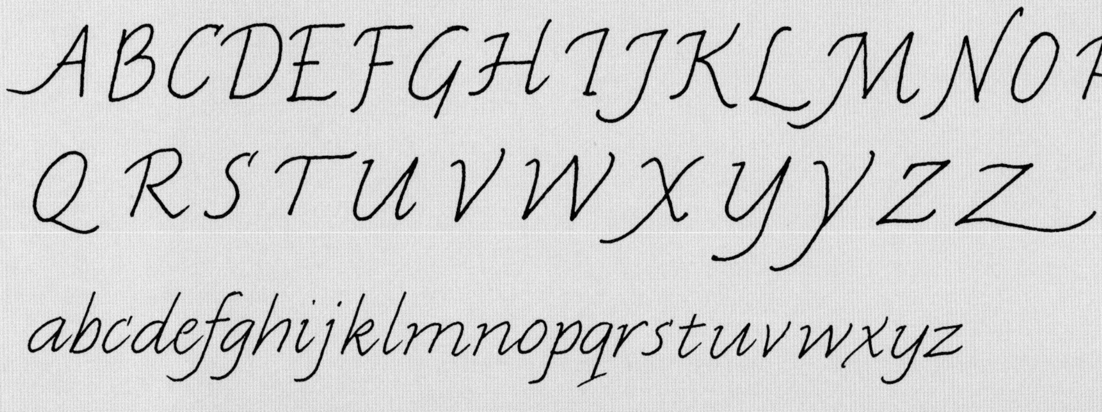

ABCDEFGHIJKLMNOP
QRSTUVWXYZ

abcdefghijklmnopqrstuvwxyz

ABCDEFGHIJKLMNOP
QRSTUVWXYYZZ

abcdefghijklmnopqrstuvwxyz

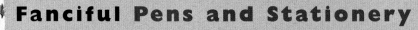

Fanciful Pens and Stationery

If you don't have beautiful penmanship, don't despair. An easy and fun way to make a letter look great is to use colorful pens and decorative stationery. The fact that you selected a distinctive pen and chose (or made!) stationery will demonstrate that letter writing is a special and important activity for you.

Pens and Writing Implements

Your choice of pen can make a big difference in the clarity of your writing, the length of your letters, and your pleasure in corresponding. The ideal pen dances across the page and doesn't drag or skip out of control, jealously insisting that you pay attention to it rather than the thoughts you wish to convey.

Some people like a writing implement that has a rigid fine point, while others prefer a pen that feels resilient and effortlessly lays down a broad line of ink. The way you hold a pen and the pressure you exert on it also influence its performance. The best way to find a pen that pleases you is to write with several kinds and compare them.

There is a veritable smorgasbord of pens available, such as ballpoints, gel writers, fountain pens, brush pens, and dual-point felt-tip pens. They come in myriad colors ranging from earth tones to delicate pastels to fluorescent and metallic inks ideal for writing on black paper.

For more formal or romantic letters, you can use elegant pens with steel or glass points that you dip into black or colored ink. Quill pens, the original pens made from goose feathers and used as early as the 16th century, can still be purchased but must be trimmed to an appropriate writing angle and are prone to wear.

To produce the thin and thick lines characteristic of calligraphy, use broad-edged pens with square-edged nibs, fountain pens, or chisel-edged markers. To write with them, you must constantly hold the pen at a 45-degree angle. If you try to manipulate the pen, you won't be able to write with the entire edge of the nib and you'll lose the thin/thick effect.

A special pen and some
colorful ink can help set letter writing apart from other tasks.

Decorative Stationery

There is a wide range of beautiful papers available in stationery shops and through paper and art-supply catalogs that are perfect for intimate correspondence or formal letter writing. Beautiful imported and handmade papers come in many colors, weights, and textures; with deckle edges; and embedded with ferns, flowers, ribbons, pine needles, bark, bits of currency, recycled paper, and some colored fibers.

In addition, you can purchase cards made from handmade and recycled papers in white or colored stock, which can be decorated with many of the techniques outlined in this book. Another option is to make your own paper or purchase large sheets of paper and cut them down in size to make your own cards and notes.

To give stationery a decorative edge, you can use edging scissors or a rolling trimmer with decorative blades. To approximate the deckle edge found on handmade paper, tear your paper over the serrated edge of an Art Deckle ruler or use a paintbrush to wet the paper with a thin line of water, then pull the paper apart or tear it against a conventional ruler.

Each type of paper accepts ink differently and you'll want to experiment to find the proper pen to use with each one. If you use the wrong pen, the writing will show a pebbly line as the pen bumps across the writing surface. A pen with a narrow nib may cause hesitation problems when used over highly ribbed stationery. You may also find that while many handmade papers will accept ballpoints and roller balls, liquid ink will bleed into some papers and make it impossible to write on them.

Even if they can't be written on successfully, many heavily embossed, textured, and exotic handmade papers can be used as great backgrounds or borders for letters written on pieces of plain paper. Exotic papers are also very useful for making collage accents for your cards and envelopes. You can often order sample packets of papers so that you can feel the textures and see how they respond to your pens.

It's easy to make your own card with a few basic tools.

HOW TO MAKE A CARD

Find the paper's grain. All machine-made papers have a grain — the direction in which the fibers line up. (Handmade papers, because their fibers are randomly distributed, have no grain.) It's important to determine the grain of the paper that you use for a card because you'll need to fold it with the grain. Otherwise, the paper may resist or crack when you fold it. Test for the grain in a sheet of paper by attempting to bend it in half. If it collapses easily, you're bending with the grain. If it resists, you're bending across the grain.

Prepare the paper for folding by scoring it with an awl, ball-tipped burnisher, or weaving needle to crease the surface. To score paper, hold a ruler with a metal edge against the desired fold line and drag the point of the tool the length of the ruler. Try to crease but not break the surface of the paper. Use a bone folder or the back of a plastic comb to apply pressure and neatly fold the paper away from, not into, the scored line.

Decorate your card with one of the techniques mentioned in this book. Then write your message and send your handcrafted letter across the miles to surprise and delight a friend.

*L*etters to a Friend

Although most of us have many acquaintances we know through business or social groups, the people we value most in our lives, our close friends, may be few in number. These are the people with whom we feel a *special bond* and with whom we can trust our innermost thoughts and secrets.

It's easy to assume that time will never erode the closeness we feel; that when we meet a friend at the airport after a five-year absence, we will *feel like college roommates again.* But life changes can create distance in a relationship, and even the closest of friendships require nurturing to be kept alive.

It is a terrible thing that people will not write unless they have materials to make a long letter, when three words would be so acceptable.

Thomas Jefferson to a friend, 1801

Sharing handwritten letters is one of the best ways to cultivate and maintain a friendship. Through letters, we can always be there to cheer each other on during joyful times and to offer comfort when facing misfortune. A letter can be read, tucked away, and reread later to allow friends to visit, console, and make each other laugh again. When we correspond with friends regularly, even gray, lonely days can be brightened by putting pen to paper to recount a shared memory or, if we're lucky, simply by checking the mail.

SUGGESTED ENCLOSURES

Tucking a small surprise with your letter into the envelope can add to the gift of the letter itself. If you keep your friend's personality and interests in mind, or think about what activities helped your special friendship flower, you'll come up with many things to include.

For instance, if your friend enjoys gardening, you might send seeds from some of your favorite perennials. Each spring, your friend will be reminded of the plants that you, too, may be enjoying at the same moment. Seeds from beautiful blue forget-me-nots are an ideal choice. (If you make paper, you can embed the seeds in the stationery and ask your friend to plant the letter.)

A handmade leaf-printed bookmark is an ideal enclosure for a friend who loves reading. It will serve as a reminder of your closeness when your friend sleepily turns in for the night after finishing another chapter. If you and your friend once spent Sunday mornings sipping cappuccino and working on the *New York Times* crossword puzzle, don't let the miles that separate you ruin the fun. You can mail the puzzle back and forth with a short letter and a promise to fill in 10 or so answers when it's your turn.

A beautiful bookmark is a great enclosure for someone who enjoys reading.

Ideas to Inspire Those with Letter Writer's Block

If you've spent so much of your creative energy preparing the special paper and picking the right pen for your letter that you're unsure of what to write about, try one of these suggestions:

- **Focus on your friend's interests** and recall your recent experiences together. You might begin a letter by saying, "I came upon a book/movie/quotation/piece of music I think you would enjoy."

- **Focus on your news.** Just a day in your life can be interesting (especially to someone who loves you) if you describe it fully. Relate how the waves break against the dock outside the beach house, the contortions of the squirrel at the bird feeder, or the colorful street vendors selling vegetables near your apartment.

- **Tell a story.** Did you do something silly lately that, though embarrassing at the time, will make your friend laugh?

- **Rekindle the past** by recounting an experience you shared with your friend. Did you vacation together, take a course together, or meet in an unusual way? Remembering something that your friend accomplished or is proud of would also be a good way to start a letter.

- **Mention why you miss your friend.** Maybe your friend was a great cook or a perfect biking partner, or you engaged in film critiques after a movie, or your thoughts were always in tune. Everyone likes to be reminded that there is something unique that he or she brings to a friendship, and it's wonderful to revisit the compliment in a letter.

Stationery embedded with forget-me-not seeds can be planted directly in the garden.

Creating **Special** Stationery

Just a few words written on a scrap of paper can be a welcome surprise in the mailbox, but taking the time to create special stationery based on your shared interests or memories can show friends that they are an important part of your life. The projects that follow are easy to do and require very little time.

MEMORABILIA STATIONERY

Use maps, sheet music, or old photos to create novel and inexpensive stationery that will roll back the years and remind your friend of the happy memories and adventures you have shared. Old and new guidebooks can provide you with maps of places you and your friend once visited together. Special music that evokes an era or favorite place or photos tucked away in an album can provide warm memories. If you have saved a place mat or a menu from a favorite restaurant you and your friend frequented, that, too, can be turned into amusing stationery.

Cut out pieces of the map or music to paste on a card or make a border for your stationery. Or, have a copy shop reduce or enlarge an old photo on a color copier and use the paper as personal stationery by writing your letter on the back. If you don't mind parting with it, write your letter on the actual dog-eared map or menu from long ago. Add gold stars on the map to highlight the places you mention in the letter, such as the town where you found the sleepy little inn and rented bicycles, boarded the Orient Express, or narrowly escaped bandits.

Liliana,

Isn't it time we took another trip together? The last vacation was just a trial run for a really big adventure. How about Indonesia next time? I know it was close, but I still think I get the prize for having the worst sense of direction. Thank goodness you brought the guidebooks!

Lost without you,
Deborah

Dear Sylvia,

I redid the old photo album last week and came upon this picture of two bathing beauties. It seems like just yesterday we were enjoying the beach and working on our tans without a thought about possible sun damage. Now the children are grown, the wrinkles have appeared, and you know what? It was worth it. Those lazy summer days with you were some of my happiest.

Let's get together soon.

Warm regards,
Cynthia

DEAR JOSEPH

REMEMBER THE PEKING GARDEN RESTAURANT WE HUNG OUT IN DURING OUR COLLEGE DAYS? I SAVED A MENU FROM OUR LAST VISIT THERE. AS I RECALL, YOUR FORTUNE COOKIE SAID YOU'D MEET A BEAUTIFUL AND MYSTERIOUS WOMAN. NOT ONLY DID YOU MEET HER— YOU MARRIED HER! SO HOW ABOUT INTRODUCING HER TO LINDA AND ME? OUR TREAT — YOU PICK THE RESTAURANT.

YOUR OLD FRENCH CLUB BUDDY,
PIERRE (AKA PETER)

LEAF PRINTING

Whether your friend is a tree surgeon or a backyard gardener, enjoys walking in the woods, or just admires beautifully decorated paper, sending a letter on leaf-printed stationery is sure to be appreciated. You can create a border of leaf prints and reserve the open area for letter writing, or you can print an entire sheet of stationery and attach the pages of your completed letter to the center of the decorated paper with dry adhesive or a ribbon tie. If your stationery paper is thin, the leaf print below it can show through, creating a lovely muted ghost image. This technique will also ensure that if you make a mistake in writing or in printing the stationery, you won't have to start over.

To make leaf prints, you'll need:

- Scissors
- Leaves
- Plant press
- Sheet of glass or Plexiglas
- Raised rubber-stamp ink pads
- Brush pens
- Tweezers (optional)
- Printing paper
- Scrap paper

MANY LEAVES from wild and cultivated plants with textured surfaces and veins will yield a good image. (Beware of poison oak and poison ivy.) Most can be plucked from the plant and printed as is. Those that need flattening can be placed in a purchased plant press or between the pages of a heavy book for a few hours to flatten them and remove some of their moisture.

Trim the stem as desired and place a leaf on the glass or Plexiglas. Press a stamp pad against the leaf or stroke it with a brush pen to coat it with color. Using your fingers or tweezers, place the leaf ink side down on the printing paper (most papers that are suitable for stationery will work just fine) and cover it with a piece of scrap paper. Use your fingers to gently press and rub it down to make the print. Then carefully remove the leaf and set it aside to be inked for another print.

Almost any kind of leaf with a textured surface can be coated with ink and used to create colorful stationery.

Wells, UK
July 23

Dear Deborah,

Visiting the tiny city of Wells in the southwest of England reminds me of the beauty and charm of our New England— the friendly small town feeling, smiling faces, and lovely shops. Of course, the sense of history here far exceeds that in the U.S. Ancient civilizations still have a strong presence that is carefully culti- vated and preserved.

Wells Cathedral is magnificent! We had a tour of the Cathedral and Bishops Palace today. Bright sun streamed through monumental stained glass windows illuminating fantastic statues and carvings. Gardens surrounding the palace contain breathtaking vistas, intimate nooks and ornamental pathways. My favorite plants were Lady's mantle and lavender, which seemed to grow so much larger than in my garden. I picked up a few sprigs from the ground for my journal.

Every home and shop has a little garden of it's own, even if there's only room for a few pots of impatiens — called dizzy lizzies. Wonderful!

All my best & will see you soon,

Laura

Dear Sally,

    I hope you are well and enjoying an early spring in your new home. It was warm enough in State College yesterday for a nostalgic hike up Nittany Mountain. Remember our early-morning expedition in search of trout lilies and ferns for your terrarium when we disturbed the pileated woodpecker? What a treat to finally see one! Then, of course, there was the day we went blueberry picking and discovered how Bear Meadows got its name.

    It's always wonderful to recall the great adventures we shared tramping through the woods and fields near the cabin, but a little sad too. I miss you. Please write and tell me all about your new life.

    Have you seen the northern lights yet?

    Much love,

      Anna

Love Letters

Love letters are a special kind of correspondence, the ultimate "letter from the heart." A love letter to someone who returns your affection may be fairly easy to write. You may intuitively know how intimate or suggestive your words can be and, if you are secure in your relationship, you needn't fear having your affections rebuffed. The love letter announcing your affection is more difficult and risky to write, but an absolute *delight* to receive. What could be more exciting than having an admirer with whom you are smitten confess his or her romantic feelings for *you*?

> *You are always new.*
> *The last of your kisses*
> *was ever the sweetest;*
> *the last smile the bright-*
> *est; the last movement*
> *the gracefulest.*
>
> John Keats
> to Fanny Brown, 1819

Romantic and Creative Missives

In addition to cementing a bond between two lovers who live thousands of miles apart, love letters can renew a relationship that has become stale. Married couples often find that their lives together become predictable to the point of boredom. Nothing breaks up the routine like finding a love letter where the grocery list is usually kept.

Getting Inspired

If you're out of practice or, just like everyone else these days, living your life in high-speed mode, writing a love letter can seem alien and the words forced, even if you are sincere. To get into a more romantic mood, choose a quiet spot and listen to soft music. Use a special antique pen and beautiful paper or write by candlelight while sipping fine wine.

A walk in the woods or in a park may also help transport you from the frenzy of your everyday life to a slower, more thoughtful pace, freeing you to express your emotions more fully. You might revisit a romantic spot, such as the little café across town or the rustic cabin in the mountains you and your lover once frequented, to rekindle your passion. If you describe your surroundings and recount your feelings when you were last together, your letter can take your lover back there with you.

Writing the Letter

Are you unsure of what to write to someone you see or talk to every day? Maybe you'll want to recall the soft Irish sweater your lover was wearing when he last embraced you, or something charming she said on your last date. By mentioning these little details in your letter, you'll prove that you delight in your love and savor his or her every word and action.

A variety of textured and hand-decorated papers make a lovely border for this card.

A few sentences focusing on the unique and endearing gestures that you love about your chosen one — the way he cocks his head when asking a question or the way she tucks her hair behind her ear before answering one — can demonstrate your attentiveness and devotion. Your letter might point out how the joy of being in love has heightened your senses and made you notice every charming thing your lover does.

A warm and loving letter may focus on your dreams for the near or distant future, your impending marriage, or your hope for a family one day. An erotic and passionate letter might contain your fantasies about your next romantic rendezvous at the seaside resort where you met. If you write about your passion for your lover, use metaphors rather than scorching graphic images. That way, your letters can be tied in satin ribbons and savored unblushingly by both of you in your old age and by your descendants in years to come.

Dearest,
    The wisteria is more fragrant and the lark's call more melodious because of you. I long to hear your footsteps on the stairs.
            I love you

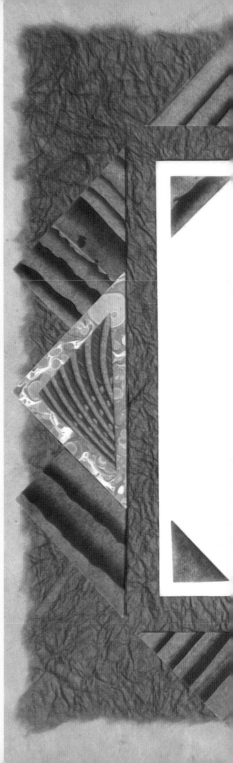

SUGGESTED ENCLOSURES

Love letters often contain a small memento that can be placed near a photo of the beloved on a dresser. You might slip a lock of your hair, some flower petals, or a packet of scented bubble bath into the envelope along with the letter.

Another idea is to make a certificate for a sensuous experience, such as a massage or a weekend at a spa. A collage of overlapping triangles cut from both decorative and plain papers could serve as a border for the message.

This certificate entitles one handsome husband to a romantic weekend at the Seven Mountains Spa with someone who loves him very much.

Creative Delivery Options

If you live miles from your lover, your letter will most likely be sent through the mail. But if you and your lover live together, you can explore more interesting ways to deliver a letter. You can slip it into a briefcase, purse, or lunch box to be discovered and relished as a surprise later in the day.

If you're going away for a weekend, you might leave the letter on top of your mate's pillow to be found at bedtime, or in the shower to be found the next morning. If your lover is leaving on a trip, you can tuck the letter into a suitcase, shaving kit, or cosmetic bag to be discovered when far from home. If you can sneak a love letter under the windshield wiper of your lover's car in a garage or business parking lot, she may be a bit embarrassed at such a public posting but will also be delighted by the surprise.

I look down the tracks and see you coming — and out of every haze and mist your darling rumpled trousers are hurrying to me.

Zelda Fitzgerald
to F. Scott Fitzgerald, 1920

Creating Special Stationery

A sure way to let your lover know he is always in your thoughts is to write a note on a napkin from a party or dinner you had to attend without him. Your message might read, "The party is elegant, but the champagne and view of the Rhine are nothing without you." If you are writing on purchased paper, you can lightly scent it with your signature perfume or cologne by using your fingertips to apply some to the back of the letter or the inside of the envelope.

Sheer fabric leaves, heart-shaped trinkets, glittery hearts, and a special stamp spill out from a note to a lover.

HANDMADE PAPER

You can create romantic stationery by producing your own handmade paper with embedded flower petals. With a simple papermaking kit (see Supply Sources), recycled paper, a blender, and flower petals, you can make your own special paper in minutes. You can also add essential oils for a customized fragrance. If you prefer to purchase rather than make your own paper, specialty stationery stores and art-supply catalogs offer a wide selection of papers. Either way, writing on a sheet of paper sprinkled with flowers can make the love message seem all the more romantic.

PRESSED-FLOWER PAPER

You can easily decorate purchased stationery with pressed flowers you've picked while on a walk with your lover. You can invest in a flower press or use an old telephone directory. Simply brush any dirt off the flowers with an artist's brush. Open a telephone directory ½-inch from the bottom and lay a flower flat on the page. Carefully cover it with another ½-inch thickness of pages and insert another flower on that page. After all the flowers are tucked in, close the directory and weight the top with a couple of heavy books.

Once the flowers have dried, brush a light coat of white glue on their backs and press them into place on your letter to create a beautiful accent. If you don't want to press your own plants, many companies sell flowers and leaves that can be grouped together to form casual or formal designs.

Scenting stationery with your perfume is especially intriguing. Apply some with your fingertips to the back of the letter or the inside of the envelope.

Dearest,

the weather is
more fragrant and the
larks call more melodious
because of you. I long
to hear your footsteps
on the stairs again.

I love you.

Diane

Embossing

You can use brass stencils to easily create the sophisticated raised patterns so often seen on wedding stationery. Embossing produces elegant borders and accents for your love letters. An embossed lover's knot can make a stunning decoration for a trifold card fastened with sealing wax. You might repeat a phrase, such as "Our love is never ending," and print the words in a border around the embossed design to further embellish the card front. You can create an embossing by pressing paper into the corners of the stencil only, making a subtle design to complement a simple message.

POSITION THE BRASS STENCIL on the front of the paper and secure it with removable tape. (If you are making a card, fold the paper first, so you can see exactly where to place the stencil and ensure that the embossing appears on the correct card flap and in the appropriate position.)

Invert the paper and stencil and place them stencil side down over a light box or against a sunny window. Work on the back of the paper and use your stylus or ball burnisher to press the paper into the illuminated openings. Emboss around the edges of the design to raise the entire pattern. As you work, turn the stencil and attached paper to thoroughly emboss all parts of the design. It will be almost impossible to retape the stencil in position if you remove it before the embossing is completed.

For embossing paper, you'll need:

- Brass stencil bearing a decorative cut pattern

- Handmade or purchased medium-weight paper in white or light colors

- Removable tape

- Light box or sunny window

- Medium-tipped stylus or ball burnisher from a crafts-supply store

You can easily create a wide range of embossed stationery with a brass stencil, a light box, and a stylus.

Thank-You Cards and Letters

A *card or letter* expressing your thanks to a person who has given you a gift, whether it be time, advice, or something tangible, is always appreciated, even if you have offered thanks in person already.

Although most thank-you letters should be written as soon as possible after a gift is received, there are some types of acknowledgements that are *most appreciated* years later. As an adult, you may realize that certain people, such as your parents or a teacher, had a profound effect on you.

Lizzie and I will ever think of you at our soup; and I shall always pour out a libation from the tureen to the angelic donor, before helping a mere vulgar broth-bidding mortal like myself.

Herman Melville thanking his cousin, Catherine Lansing, for a soup ladle, 1872

Thank You to a Parent or Mentor

Letters to adults who have made a difference in your life — perhaps a teacher, an author, or member of the clergy who helped give your life direction — are fulfilling to write and wonderful to receive. Letting people know they have made a lasting impression on you can validate their life's work and encourage them to continue giving to others.

Another letter that can be sent long after a gift is received is a thank-you letter to your parents. This may be the most meaningful letter you ever write. I've always been happy that I sent such a letter to my parents. I know how much it meant to them, for after their deaths, I found my letter in their safe-deposit box along with precious jewelry and important legal documents.

You might thank your parents for raising you and supporting your decision to give up the high school chess club in favor of baton-twirling lessons. If you were part of a hopelessly amateur garage band that played especially loud music, monopolized the family phone, or cut math classes, you may thank them for putting up with your teenage interests and youthful indiscretions.

Parents who helped fund your college education are especially deserving of thanks, as are those who, after years of tuition payments, still support your desire to be a freelance photographer instead of the research psychologist you were trained to become.

Dear Mom and Dad,

I am so lucky to have you as parents! When you came to my photography show at the Marshalton Gallery and told me that you were proud of my creative success, it was one of the finest and warmest moments of my life. It is wonderful to know that your love and respect is with me even if I'm not the research psychologist we all thought I would be.

Thanks for helping me follow my dreams.

Kate

SUGGESTED ENCLOSURES

It's fun to include a humorous enclosure in a thank-you letter to parents. A prepaid phone card might be included with a letter in which you apologize for all the collect calls you made. You might create an old-fashioned report card for them and give them A's in areas such as "listening skills," "helpfulness," and "ability to remain cheerful when faced with a difficult task."

Mom & Dad's Report Card

A+ Listen well ★

A+ Help others build confidence ★

A+ Remain cheerful when faced with difficult tasks

A+ Set a great example for others

A+ ★ Always have time to be supportive

In appreciation for feeding me
and
for making me eat my vegetables
this certificate entitles

John and Ann Vogel

to one day's work
helping to weed the summer garden.

This certificate is void if okra is planted.

BEANS

CUCUMBERS

PUMPKIN

Lettuce

PEAS

OKRA

KEEPSAKE CERTIFICATES

An easy and thoughtful way to show your appreciation is to create a keepsake certificate to help your parents plant a summer garden, paint a spare room, wash and wax the family car, or train the family dog.

CUT YOUR CERTIFICATE PAPER TO SIZE with a paper cutter or trim it with an X-Acto knife and a ruler with a metal cutting edge. Work over a cutting mat, and holding your knife upright, slide it against the metal edge as you pull the blade toward you. Use colored pencils, gel pens, or felt-tip markers to create a border for your promissory note.

If your drawing ability is still evolving, you can trace pictures instead. To do this, trace the design you wish to copy. Use a soft pencil to scribble over the back of the traced image to deposit pencil carbon on the reverse side of the tracing paper. Invert the tracing paper so that the carbon side is *face down* on your certificate and trace the images again with a sharp pencil. When you remove the tracing paper, you'll find that a faint image appears on your promissory note. Color in the image with colored pencils, markers, gel pens, or watercolor paints to form a border for a message.

A promise to help weed the garden is a thoughtful way to show appreciation.

Dear Mrs. Morrison,   June 1

Some 20 years ago I was a boy of seven whom you probably remember as a constant fixture in your bakery. You were kind enough to let me eat the broken cookies, tie string around the donut boxes, and watch you make and decorate marvelous five-tiered wedding cakes. I wanted you to know that your kindness and artistry made a big impression on me.

I recently graduated from the Culinary Institute of America and will soon become a pastry chef at Maison Camille, a 4-star restaurant in Seattle, Washington.

With best wishes
and sincere thanks, Giles

DECORATIVE BORDERS

An easy way to make a card or letter look like a special certificate is to place a decorative border around the periphery of the paper. This is a great technique if you want to make your own stationery and then use a few different types of borders to vary the way you set off your creations.

CUT YOUR PAPER or stationery to size with a paper cutter or use an X-Acto knife and a metal-edged ruler over a cutting mat. Use some of the decorative punches available at craft stores to create open designs in the corners of your stationery or repeatedly punch designs just inside all four edges of a sheet of paper. Use dry adhesive to affix the punched paper to a colored sheet of paper so that flashes of color from the second sheet show through the first.

Add interest by layering and adhering smaller sheets of paper over progressively larger ones, which will create colorful borders. Use a ruler and pencil to measure and lightly mark where layered sheets should be placed. Decorate the paper with edging scissors or a paper trimmer with a decorative blade.

Another way to make a decorative edge that enhances the look of layered papers is to tear the edge of the paper over the serrated edge of an Art Deckle ruler. This will give your stationery a feathery look that resembles the deckle edge found on handmade paper. When your stationery's border design is complete, write the letter or glue a previously written letter in place.

To create decorative borders, you'll need:

- Drawing paper or stationery in various colors
- Paper cutter
- X-Acto knife with #11 blade
- Ruler with a metal cutting edge
- Cutting mat
- Decorative punches
- Corner punches
- Roll-on dry adhesive or archival mounting film (*not* rubber cement)
- Pencil
- Edging scissors
- Paper trimmer with decorative cutting blades (optional)
- Art Deckle ruler

Special scissors make a fanciful edge on ordinary stationery printed from your computer.

Thank You for a Gift

A thank-you note acknowledging a birthday, holiday, or wedding gift is a necessity, and it is considered rude to fail to send one. If the gift was sent rather than delivered in person, the donor may think the present was lost in the mail if you don't respond promptly. Your note can be short and to the point or lavish with praise to show your appreciation. If the gift is off the mark, mention the present and thank the giver for his or her thoughtfulness. If you love the gift as well as the gesture, mention how you plan to use it or how well it complements your wardrobe or decor. If the gift is money, it's considered polite to mention what you bought with it or how you plan to use it. That way, the giver will feel a part of your life.

SUGGESTED ENCLOSURES

A photo of you wearing your new scarf or using your new serving tray at a backyard barbecue makes a good letter enclosure. A copy of a fabulous dessert recipe you discovered in your new cookbook or a favorable book review of the novel given to you would also be appreciated. A lottery ticket wrapped in a note saying, "I feel so lucky to know you — here's hoping you have good luck, too" would be fun to discover in a thank-you note.

To make a woven card, you'll need:

- Cutting mat
- X-Acto knife with #11 blade
- Cover-weight drawing paper or cardstock
- Pencil
- Ruler with metal cutting edge
- Awl or weaving needle
- Wrapping paper
- Two sheets of colored drawing paper or cardstock that coordinate with the wrapping paper
- Paper punch
- White glue
- Toothpick to use as glue applicator
- Dry adhesive

WOVEN CARDS

If you make a woven thank-you card incorporating strips of the wrapping paper that a birthday, holiday, shower, or wedding gift came in, you can let the giver know that you appreciated not only the gift but the choice of the wrapping paper, too.

You can make variations of this card by changing the paper's dimensions, adding more or fewer slits, and following different weaving patterns. Your warp (crosswise slits) can be cut in wavy or zigzag shapes, rather than straight lines, and need not be equidistant from one another. Your weft (lenghtwise strips) can be made of materials such as ribbons and strips of paper cut with edging scissors. The weft ends can extend freely or be glued to the back of the weaving. By cutting slits in purchased stationery and weaving beautiful decorative papers through them, you can easily add a small woven accent to any letter.

THERE ARE TWO COMPONENTS to making this card: creating the basic card and creating the weaving. After both are completed, you will attach them to each other. To create the card, use the cutting mat and the X-Acto knife to cut a piece of drawing paper or cardstock 5¾ inches by 11 inches. Then, using an awl or a weaving needle, drag the point of the tool against the edge of a ruler to score, or slightly crease, the paper for folding. Score at the five-inch mark to create a card that's slightly longer in the back than in the front. Fold the card.

To create the weaving, start with a 3¼-inch square of drawing paper and draw horizontal and vertical lines ¼ inch in from the edges. These lines will determine the height and positioning of your weaving slits. Use the ruler and X-Acto knife to make your first vertical slit ¼ inch in from the edge of the paper. The slit will begin on the horizontal line you just drew, ¼ inch down from the top of the paper, and end ¼ inch in from the bottom. Measure ½ inch beyond the first slit and draw and cut another parallel slit. Continue making four more parallel slits to give you a total of six slits that will function as a stationery warp for your weaving.

Cut three strips of wrapping paper ½ inch wide and 6 or 7 inches long. Cut three strips of colored drawing paper ¼ inch wide and 6 or 7 inches long. Weave these weft strips tabby style (over and under) in the slits you cut to create the weaving. Trim the weft ends on an angle. Punch dots of plain paper and wrapping paper and use a toothpick applicator to glue them to the card to decorate the front of the weaving.

Cut two progressively larger squares of paper and adhere them to each other and to the woven panel with dry adhesive. Adhere the woven panel to the card front with dry adhesive. Then adhere a strip of wrapping paper along the bottom of the card on the longer side.

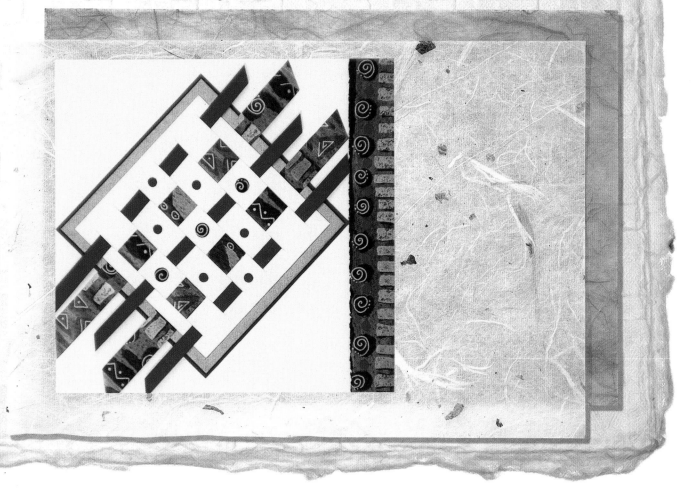

The Bread-and-Butter Thank-You Card

The bread-and-butter thank-you card, which is expected from overnight guests, can be sent through the mail or left on a dresser to surprise your hosts when they change the linens in the guest room. You can show your appreciation in your note by mentioning how comfortable and welcome you felt at your hosts' home.

If a special dinner was prepared for you or if you were taken out to dinner, you might mention how delicious the meal was and how much you enjoyed the dinner conversation. Your card might also compliment your hosts on their lovely home, beautiful landscaping, well-behaved children, or friendly pets.

Many thanks for your kindness.

Snapshots of your friends' children or pets are nice to send after a visit.

SUGGESTED ENCLOSURES

An appropriate enclosure for a card sent through the mail would be a candid snapshot of the hosts' children or pets or a photo of you with your hosts. You might also send some photos of a beautiful place you visited together.

Another idea is to enclose a standing invitation to visit you, which could be written on a piece of cardstock folded so that it actually stands. A movie review of a film you saw together during your visit or a magazine article about items your friends may collect would also be an appreciated surprise.

QUILLING

A quilled, or filigree, thank-you card is especially beautiful. Don't be surprised if you see it framed and hanging in the guest room when you next visit. Quilling is not as fragile as it looks, and if you write "hand stamp" on the envelope, your card will travel safely through the mail.

There are two types of quilled coil shapes: open and closed. An open coil is not secured with glue, but is allowed to open and expand. It often has a long, graceful arching tail. In a closed coil, the end of the quilling strip is glued down, preventing the coil from expanding.

You can make endless designs by varying the position of the basic quilled shapes. Try making a border of daisies around the entire front of the card, changing the size of the coils. Or arrange the coils to form an abstract rather than a representational design.

To make quilled cards, you'll need:

- Pack of ⅛- or ¹⁄₁₆-inch-wide quilling paper, or cut your own strips from medium-weight paper
- Quilling tool or round toothpick as a substitute
- White glue
- Toothpick to use as glue applicator
- Wax paper
- Prefolded card
- ¹⁄₁₆-inch ribbon (optional)

TO ROLL A BASIC CLOSED COIL, tear off a 4-inch strip of quilling paper and wind the cut end around a quilling tool. Use your thumb and forefinger to roll the paper toward you so that each round stacks neatly on top of the previous one. Remove the coil from the tool, let it expand just a bit, apply a dot of glue to the loose end with a toothpick, and secure it to the loosely rolled coil.

To make a pegged shape, roll a tight coil and glue the end down before removing it from the quilling tool. To create a teardrop form, pinch one side of a loose coil. To make an eye-shaped coil, gently pinch both sides of a loose coil. To make a half-moon shape, press down on top of a loose coil to flatten and slightly indent it.

Construct the vines to which the quilled shapes are attached by gluing strips of quilling paper together. Gently curve them by wrapping them around your finger. Position them on top of a piece of wax paper. Using a toothpick and a tiny bit of glue, add small open coils or scrolls here and there. Then glue the assorted quilled shapes to the vine and to each other to form leaves and flowers.

When the glue has dried, remove your quilling forms from the wax paper, add small dots of glue to the back of the designs, and place them in position on the front of the prefolded card. Add a narrow ribbon, if desired, tacking it in place with tiny dots of glue.

We had a lovely time visiting your home last weekend. Many thanks, Maggie and Norm

Letters to Children

Writing to children brings back your own childhood memories. And getting a letter from a child with an appreciation for such things as ladybugs, board games, and knock-knock jokes can be an invigorating reminder to stop taking life so seriously.

Some people intuitively know how to write letters to children that will *elicit giggles* or genuine interest. For many of us, though, writing to children with whom we don't spend a lot of time can be tricky. It's important to know how to address various age groups without talking down to them or using words that are so hopelessly outdated you can almost hear the groans when they read the letter. But there is always hope that children will continue the correspondence as they get older and become *life-long friends*.

You are as hard to forget as you are soft to roll down a hill with. What fun it was! Only so prickly I thought I had a porcupine in one pocket and a hedgehog in the other. The next time, before we kiss the earth we will have its face well shaved.

Thomas Hood
to one of his doctor's
young daughters, 1844

Getting Inspired

If you recently shared an experience with children, you can write about your adventures together to help build a bond with them. Children always appreciate silliness, and if you can combine that with wordplay, your letter is bound to be appreciated. If they are relatives or the children of a friend you recently visited, you probably know what interests them and makes them laugh.

Your letter can ask how their last softball game went or what they plan to be for Halloween. If you inquire about school, camp, favorite songs, hobbies, or books, the children will have something to write back to you about. If they have a pet, you might ask about it and describe some of the funny things *your* pet has done lately. You might watch some of the children's favorite television shows or read a book they are also reading, so that you can discuss the characters and the plot.

Young children might like drawing and sending pictures of their favorite toys, pets, or themselves at play — especially if they know you will be posting them on your refrigerator. Another idea that can help solidify a relationship with children (after checking with the parents) is to send them an inexpensive camera so they can send you photos they snap themselves.

To encourage shy children to write to you, engage them in an imaginary correspondence with your dog, cat, or hamster. They'll know it's pretend but will be delighted to receive the letters. Plus, you'll have great fun writing to them.

Woof Laura,

Thank you for brushing and petting me on Saturday. Don't you think I'm the biggest dog ever? Oops! I have to go bark at the postman!

Now I'm back. Do you know where my biscuits are kept? I can play Frisbee with you and jump so high. I'll look very small until I come back down again.

Hoping to sniff you soon,
Jake, the very big husky

Children love to enclose their artwork with letters.

INSPIRING CHILDREN

You can help your children grow into adults who enjoy letter writing by showing them how much fun it can be. Share your excitement with your children when you receive a letter by reading parts of it to them. When you write back to a friend or relative, include drawings by your children or let them add a line or two to your letter. You can include children too young to write by letting them tell you what they would like to say and writing it for them.

Children always enjoy arts and crafts, and creating special stationery and letter enclosures can be an ongoing rainy-day project. Many of the projects in this book are easy enough for children to enjoy with a little help from an adult. You can also give colorful cards or stationery on holidays and birthdays to encourage children to send thank-you notes for the gifts they have received. Finally, rather than correcting a young child's note, let the inevitable misspelled words and creative grammar pass so that letter writing is fun and not a cause for criticism.

Creating Special Stationery

It's a little-known fact that just about anything can be used as stationery if you put the proper postage on it. I remember being delighted to receive a letter written on a little crate of candy oranges when my favorite uncle went to Florida. Your child correspondent will receive your letter in openmouthed amazement if you write it on something unconventional and send it in the mail. For example, you can write a birthday card on a folded party hat and a Halloween card on a paper mask. Or try writing a message on a sturdy leaf to signify the fall season and back-to-school days. You can even send a piece of wood in the mail with the message:

Party hats, birch bark, wood, and a paper mask become stationery with just a little creativity.

Wood you please write?

I miss you.

SUGGESTED ENCLOSURES

Young children love to receive surprise enclosures in letters. You might send something as simple as a beautiful feather that you found in your yard or a foreign stamp from a letter that was sent to you. If you've created special stationery for your letters, such as spattered or sponged stationery, you can include directions for spatter painting. Or slip in a compressed sponge that can be cut into a special shape, expanded in water, and dipped into paint and used as a printing device.

Popular trading cards and temporary tattoos will always be a hit, as will gift certificates for snacks at national restaurants and movie theaters. Enclosures that will encourage a child to write back could include stickers to decorate a return letter and self-addressed stamped postcards. You can also encourage an ongoing correspondence by instituting a game of tick-tack-toe. Just enclose a piece of paper with a game board drawn on it and place an X in one spot with an invitation to play.

Very young children may enjoy receiving an enclosure of a story that has gaps where words need to be filled in. It may read something like "Once there was a little _____who lived in a very wet ____." The child can read the sentence with a parent and fill in the missing words to create a story with you as you exchange letters.

Children always enjoy receiving small gifts enclosed in letters.

SHAPED CARDS

You can make a card out of vegetable, fruit, toy, animal, and other shapes a child would enjoy. A card that looks like a slice of watermelon is a delightful card to send to a child who has just gotten out of school for the summer!

USE THE COMPASS OR CIRCLE CUTTER to trace progressively larger circles in red, white, and green paper. (You can also draw circles by tracing progressively larger dishes.) Cut out the circles with scissors. Fold the paper circles in half and arrange them inside each other with green on the inside, white in the middle, and red on the outside. Measure and mark points A, B, and C on the fold, as shown in the diagram below.

Use a pamphlet-stitching pattern to join the three sheets of paper on the fold line. With a sewing needle and a piece of embroidery floss or ribbon 3½ times the height of your largest circle, sew from the outside through the center hole (B) in the stack of paper. Leave an 8-inch-long tail of cord extending from the card. Pull the ribbon through to the center of the card and up to the top hole (A). Enter that hole and pull the ribbon over the outside of the card, bypassing the center hole, and down to the bottom hole (C).

Pull the ribbon taut as you continue. Bring the ribbon through to the center of the card and then reenter the center hole (B) to bring the cord through to the outside of the card again. Position the two ends of the ribbon (the original tail and the new end you just brought through) so that they straddle the long length of ribbon running from hole A to hole C, then tie them together.

Use the black marker to draw watermelon seeds on the red paper or, if you have a punch that produces teardrop shapes, punch seeds from black paper and glue them on. Leave the stitched flaps of the watermelon open so that you can write hidden messages throughout the card as well as inside it.

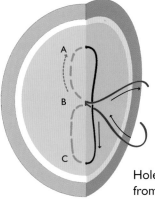

Hole B is positioned in the middle of the card. Holes A and C are eqidistant from the two ends and Hole B. Follow the arrows for stitching.

Cards shaped like favorite foods are
especially fun for children to receive.

PUZZLE LETTERS

The letter from Jake, the husky, could arrive in pieces as an unassembled puzzle. Then the child could assemble it to find that your letter is written on stationery shaped like a large dog biscuit. You can also draw or stamp pictures of paw prints or biscuits on the card or write "Jake's Bone" on the brown paper in colorful letters. You can make a puzzle card out of any simple shape. Or cut a postcard or a drawing pasted onto cardboard into puzzle pieces.

To make a dog-bone puzzle card, you'll need:

- Heavy brown drawing paper, cardstock, or blotter paper

- Ruler

- Heart-shaped cookie cutter

- Gel pen in a color light enough to show up when used on brown stationery

- Paw-print rubber stamp or stencil

- Scissors

MAKE THE OUTLINE of a large dog bone on brown paper by using the ruler and the cookie cutter to create a large rectangle with a heart at both ends. (Or you can draw one freehand.) Write your letter on the bone; decorate it with paw prints, if desired; cut out the bone; then cut the bone into several pieces. Three pieces will be enough for a very small child, while an older one can probably assemble a puzzle with considerably more divisions. Put the pieces into an envelope, mark the envelope "hand stamp," and send it off.

A postcard can be cut into puzzle shapes and assembled by young readers.

A dog bone card can be made from heavy brown paper, a ruler, and a heart-shaped cookie cutter, then trimmed into puzzle pieces.

SPATTER PAINTING

Spatter painting is a simple way to create colorful stationery. If children haven't already learned this technique in school, they'll be sure to ask you how you did it. If they have learned the technique, they'll be anxious to send you a letter showing what their painting style looks like. Since you'll no doubt spatter beyond your paper, you may want to do this project outside or work within a cardboard box.

To do spatter painting, you'll need:

- Any type of paper

- Newspaper to protect the table from paint

- Cardboard box with the top and one side removed (optional)

- Acrylic paint thinned with water

- Flat dish

- Toothbrush or vegetable brush

- Tongue depressor or ruler

PLACE YOUR STATIONERY on top of a large sheet of newspaper or scrap paper. Place them inside a cardboard box, if desired. Pour some slightly diluted acrylic paint onto the flat dish and dip the brush bristles into it. Coat the brush well, then tap off some of the paint onto extra newspaper.

Hold the brush with the bristles up and the front tipped slightly downward. Draw the tongue depressor or ruler toward you over the bristles to spatter the paint. Work closer to or farther away from the paper to vary the intensity of the spatters. When the first coat of paint is dry, spatter another color of paint.

As a variation, try placing flat leaves, keys, or paper cutouts here and there on the paper and spattering around them to create a kind of stencil design. You can also place a smaller piece of paper on top of your stationery to form a mask. After spattering and removing the smaller paper, you will be left with a sheet of stationery with a spattered border.

Spattering paint on pieces of paper is a fun way for children to make stationery.

Travel Letters and Postcards

Whether your vacation is full of adventures in an exotic land or simply a restful week or two at the beach, those toiling away at home will enjoy hearing from you and seeing or reading a description of your surroundings. Sending travel letters and postcards benefits the vacationer, too. While spinning a rack of postcards, you may find an interesting side trip you hadn't planned. It's fun to select evocative stationery and postcards of beautiful scenery and write to your friends from a little café or park *in a foreign land*. And putting your thoughts into words to vividly describe a memorable scene will help solidify your memory of a place.

The silent streets are paved with water, and you hear nothing but the dashing of the oars, and the occasional cries of the gondolieri.

Percy Bysshe Shelley
describing Venice
to Thomas Love Peacock, 1818

Travelogues

Vacation is a perfect time to slow down and absorb all of the things you are seeing and doing. And what better way to contemplate your new surroundings than by sharing your thoughts with a friend? Writing will help you appreciate your experiences and reflect on a new culture and different way of life. Even what seems like a mundane event, such as going to a market, drinking a cup of cappucino at a sidewalk café, or taking a local bus to a small village, can become an eye-opening or amusing story when you relate it to a friend.

Getting Inspired

If you keep a travel journal or at least jot down names and colorful details about places you visit during the day, you'll find it easy to remember things to write about later.

Be as descriptive as possible — your friends and family want to see the sights through your eyes. If you mention things that will interest your correspondents, they will know that you are really thinking of them and not just writing a generic greeting to be copied on every card.

For instance, don't just say, "Java is great, you'd love it here." Remember your friend's particular interests by writing, "I know a bargain hunter like you would love Java. The first person to buy a batik or a shadow puppet each morning gets a discount to bring the shop owner good luck."

Another way to show that you care is to address each letter or card by hand. It really doesn't take that long and a small address book slipped into your luggage doesn't take up much space, either. Preprinted address labels may be somewhat more convenient for the writer, but they tell the recipient that part of the "chore" was done at home.

Small mementos from a trip, when tucked inside a letter, literally bring another part of the world to the recipient.

SUGGESTED ENCLOSURES

Foreign stamps are frequently very colorful and you don't have to be a stamp collector to appreciate them. In addition to choosing one as postage, it's a nice surprise to enclose some in your letter. They're interesting to see and they make great collage materials for artistic-minded friends.

Foreign currency makes a great enclosure as well. Unlike American money, the small-denomination bills of many foreign countries depict colorful plants and wildlife. It can also be fun to send unusual and humorous advertisements on matchbooks or in magazines, as well as labels on grocery items — especially if the attempts at an English translation miss the mark.

A tape or CD of hyena howls heard during your African safari or the call to prayer you recorded at dawn in Turkey would really provide recipients with the flavor of your travels. Or perhaps a friend would enjoy a piece of Irish lace or an embroidered handkerchief from Portugal.

If you're traveling in the United States, you can usually enclose tiny shells or exotic leaves, which may be illegal to send from abroad. (Check with authorities before sending such things to or from Hawaii.) A trip to New Orleans might inspire you to send some Mardi Gras beads or a recipe for making jambalaya. A visit to Chinatown in any large American city can provide you with imported tiny fans, paper cutouts, and other folded decorations.

Creating Special Stationery

Instead of purchasing a postcard, you can send a more personal note that you've made from a photo taken during your trip. Just have your film developed in your vacation spot and attach it to a photo/postcard backing board. These boards are available at many art-supply and photo stores and contain a sticky surface covered with a slippery sheet of paper that you peel off to apply your photo.

A coaster from a pub or a piece of advertising art, such as a charming scene on a cookie or biscuit box, can also be turned into an unusual postcard by writing a message around the border. Just trim the edges of the biscuit box, glue the box to a piece of mat board, and add a message in gold pen that might read something like this: "In England and France, even the advertising is beautiful. I bet Jake would sit for one of these biscuits."

Menus from restaurants where you've dined or brochures from attractions you've visited can also be used as novel stationery. Just write your message on the margins of the brochure (add an address label if the brochure is too cluttered with type) and apply the proper postage. Although your letter won't have quite the same charm, you could slip the brochure into an envelope and send it off.

If you are traveling in the United States, you can write your message on a piece of driftwood, barnwood, or a sturdy shell and send it through the mail.

A lovely scene from a French biscuit box is turned into a unique postcard.

COLLAGES

Although most people prefer to send short notes and postcards during their travels, you can also create a more elaborate card to send once you return home. Simply save photos, brochures, ticket stubs, and other ephemera from your vacation. You can also use decorative papers you purchased in Japan, parts of rubbings you made in England, or colorful foreign currency you saved from Belize.

Create designs by gluing strips of the papers on top of or overlapping one another. Even postage stamps arranged on colorful backing papers make a beautiful collage card. Then photocopy your collage and paste it onto the front of a folded card. After you see how easy it is to make a collage card, you may want to send some originals (along with the juicy details of your vacation) to special friends. If you pack a dry-adhesive roller and some cardstock in your luggage, you may even find yourself making and sending some of these from the road.

If you save small items as you travel, it's easy to create a collage that depicts your entire trip.

To make a collage, you'll need:

- Photos, brochures, tickets, stamps, foreign money, and other flat or paper ephemera
- Dry adhesive
- Heavy watercolor paper or photo-backing board
- Prefolded card
- Colored pencils or markers
- Scissors
- X-Acto knife
- Cutting mat
- Metal-edged ruler

Collages are a fun project to do with children. Save your old magazines for additional inspiration.

ASSEMBLE SOME PAPER MEMORABILIA from your trip in coordinating colors. Using dry adhesive, paste a large item or two to the backing paper that will support your collage. You can use a piece of heavy watercolor paper or photo-backing board slightly smaller than your card front.

Tear, rather than cut, some pieces from your brochures that feature a word, part of a map, an animal, or a person in traditional dress. Tear away from the paper as you hold it, which gives it a clean ragged edge, or tear toward you to expose part of the paper's core. Decorate some of the torn edges with colored pencils or markers to accent the piece and enhance your color scheme. Use scissors to vary the shapes and sizes of the elements in your collage.

Using an X-Acto knife, a cutting mat, and a metal-edged ruler, slice into one or more of the photos and lift part of an image forward. This lets you slip another picture behind it and create dimension. Experiment by moving materials to different places and behind some of the other elements. Rotate some pieces to see how they work in a horizontal or an off-balance position. Repeat colors to keep the viewer's eye moving through the piece. Add a bright flash of a contrasting color to keep your collage exciting. Let some of the papers extend beyond the backing paper to add interest. When you are pleased with your composition, adhere the elements in place. Make color photocopies of the finished work and glue them to prefolded cards, or use the original collage as a one-of-a-kind card.

Congratulatory Cards

Everyone has sent congratulatory cards on birthdays and for other milestones. Cards containing messages or poems under which you can just sign your name are easy to find in shops nationwide. It's always great to be remembered, but it is much *nicer to read* a few handwritten lines expressing good wishes, rather than the packaged sentiments of card manufacturers.

Many of the commercial *handmade* greeting cards are blank inside, allowing the sender to compose a longer, *more personal message* to the recipient. However, despite the proliferation of gorgeous cards on the market today, the most appreciated card of all is usually the one that is created entirely by the sender.

I shouldn't be surprised if matrimony didn't do you a heap of good . . . it teaches a man to keep his temper and to remember that the earth does not revolve absolutely and eternally round his hat. Well, bless you both.

Rudyard Kipling to novelist Guy Boothby on the announcement of his impending marriage, 1893

Congratulate in Style

A congratulatory card is in order for the obvious big events, such as births and adoptions, birthdays, bar and bat mitzvahs, graduations, weddings, new homes, anniversaries, and retirements. Probably the most appreciated acknowledgement, however, is for an accomplishment or a milestone that most people would not think of observing with a card. A true measure of friendship is how interested you are in the details of another person's life. By recognizing your friend's achievements, however small and insignificant they may seem to an outsider, you'll let your friend know that you truly care.

Congratulations on your retirement to Costa Rica. It's such a beautiful country!

Love from, the Jackson family

SPECIAL EVENTS THAT DESERVE A CONGRATULATORY CARD

You can become a small but very loud cheering section by noting of your friends' accomplishments, special events they are looking forward to, or things they have done that took effort or courage. Even if humility prevents them from crowing about it, they will be thrilled to receive a card that congratulates them on:

- **Admission to the school of their choice**
- **Appearing in a local newspaper**
- **Finishing chemotherapy**
- **Getting braces off**
- **Getting a cast off**
- **Getting a promotion**
- **Getting a Web site**
- **Landscaping a yard**
- **Learning a new craft or skill**
- **Making the honor roll**
- **Overcoming a phobia**
- **Paying off a mortgage**
- **Publishing a book**
- **Quitting smoking**
- **Receiving a professional reward**
- **Remodeling a home**
- **Winning a contest**

Getting Inspired

Your card's message can be short and sweet. A more long-winded card, however, may be suitable for someone whose baseball team has just won the league play-offs. That card might contain the scores of all the games played that year to underscore the victory.

You can probably think of many events in your loved ones' lives that could be marked with special greeting cards. Perhaps a friend has been struggling to quit smoking and has finally achieved his goal or a relative has recently finished a runner's marathon. Maybe it's something as simple as getting a driver's license after several tries.

You don't have to compose a flowery poem to send good wishes to friends. Just a line or two to say that you are thinking about them on their birthday or anniversary can mean a lot. You might mention how vibrant your pal is despite reaching the big five-o or that your friends make a handsome couple.

A good way to remember important dates that occur each year is to mark them on your calendar each January first. Just transfer the dates from the previous year's calendar to the new one. Make note of special days in people's lives when you hear about them, whether directly or indirectly. Sending a surprise greeting to a casual friend is always appreciated and may lead to a stronger friendship.

A simple greeting of "happy day" is appropriate for any special occasion.

SUGGESTED ENCLOSURES

You can recognize a loved one's milestone in an even more enjoyable way by enclosing something special with your card. Even silly things can make your note more fun. For example, you might include some photocopied Monopoly money with a congratulatory note about starting a new business, paying off the mortgage, or buying a home. Your note could say, "First the house on Cedar Road, next a hotel on Park Place. Congratulations!"

A new author or a person who just got a lead role in a community play might enjoy receiving a small pocket calendar to keep track of forthcoming "celebrity appearances." A person who just got a dream sailboat or a new car might find a small outrageously colored key chain fun to receive. Tiny barrettes slipped in with congratulations on the birth of a baby girl would also make a good enclosure gift.

STENCILING

You can use brass stenciling plates, such as those for embossing, to make beautiful congratulatory cards. In time, you may want to try cutting your own stencils; but for quick and colorful greeting cards, the stenciling plates can't be beat. There is a wide range of images available, so finding the appropriate one is quite easy.

To make a stenciled card, you'll need:

- Deckle-edged or plain paper
- Edging scissors or Art Deckle ruler
- Three stencil brushes in sizes that fit the openings in your stencil (one brush for reds and yellows, one for greens and blues, and another for purples and other dark colors)
- Stencil colors or a multi-colored water-based ink stamp pad
- Paper towels
- Brass stenciling plate
- Hole punch (optional)
- Ribbon (optional)
- Decorative paper
- Prefolded card

CUT YOUR PAPER TO SIZE and give it a deckled or decorative edge. To charge your brush with color, hold it perpendicular and touch the surface of the color container with the flat edge of the applicator. Still holding your brush perpendicular, tap it against a paper towel to evenly distribute the color. The brush should be almost dry when it's used, to prevent the color from bleeding under the stencil openings and blurring the edges of your designs.

Hold the brass stencil in position over the paper and move the almost-dry brush in a circular motion, rubbing the paint into the stencil openings. Start on top of the brass plate and, using your lightest colors first, work from the edge of the plate's opening to the center, laying down a thin layer of color. It's not necessary to fill in the entire stencil opening with intense color. Sometimes a darker shade on the edges of the opening leading to a lighter concentration of color in the center of the design can be very effective.

Let your stenciled paper dry, then punch two holes in the card to insert coordinating ribbons, if desired. Glue the stenciled paper to a decorative paper and then to the front of the prefolded card to create a layered design.

Brass stenciling plates make it easy to send beautiful layered congratulatory cards.

Holidays and Special Occasions

Many people send and receive annual holiday cards, displaying them in their homes as part of their holiday decorations. The computer-generated *annual letter* is also commonly used to summarize the news of the year. Births, deaths, illnesses, job changes, vacations, and divorces are often lumped together in one letter. However, if you're a close friend, you probably know about such life changes. If you aren't, it can be embarrassing to be privy to very personal details. If you correspond regularly during the year, you won't feel obligated to send this type of letter and can *create something unique* instead.

No snow — the roads like iron — and the thermometer nearly zero and tomorrow is Xmas day! I hope it will be pleasanter weather for you than promises for us. With best wishes from my wife and myself for all that the new year brings.

Rudyard Kipling
to Sarah Orne Jewett,
December 24, 1894

Annual **Holiday Cards**

For a truly memorable holiday card, you can create a piece of artwork, write a holiday poem on paper decorated with a stamped or stenciled border design, and send photocopies or computer scans of the artwork to friends and family. You can also make a collage of family interests and photos and include quotes by family members. Then photocopy or scan the collage, add a personal note, and send it off. Another option for the holiday letter is to have each family member handwrite his or her news, then photocopy the letter.

A piece of artwork with a poem makes a very personal holiday card.

HOLIDAYS TO CELEBRATE

There are many holidays and times of year that are perfect for sending cards to bring friends up to date on your news or to wish them well. If you consider your friends' backgrounds, you will think of many holidays to recognize with a card. Friends of a specific ethnicity may enjoy a card observing a holiday taking place in their country of origin. Here are a few ideas:

- **Christmas, Hanukkah, and Kwanza**
- **Cinco de Mayo**
- **Earth Day**
- **Easter**
- **Father's Day and Mother's Day**
- **First day of a new season**
- **Grandparents' Day**
- **Groundhog Day**
- **Halloween**
- **Independence Day**
- **Memorial Day**
- **New Year's Day**
- **Rosh Hashanah**
- **Saint Patrick's Day**
- **Thanksgiving**
- **Valentine's Day**

PHOTO-FRAMES

To make a photo-frame you'll need:

- Cardstock or drawing paper, 5½" x 12¾"
- Pencil
- 3-inch heart-shaped cookie cutter
- X-Acto knife
- Cutting mat
- Hole punch (small diameter preferred)
- Ribbon
- Scissors
- Dry adhesive
- Photocopy of your mother's (or grandmother's) picture — either a recent one or a photo taken years ago
- Glue brush
- White glue
- Pressed flowers

It's hard to think of anyone more deserving of a holiday card than the mother who gave you life and lovingly cared for you throughout your early years. Your mother probably has a collection of cards you've given her tucked away for safekeeping, starting with the first crayon-adorned card you made in kindergarten. Although the ones you send now may no longer find a place on your mom's refrigerator, a unique handmade card will probably have a home in a family album and will certainly reside in your mother's heart.

A charming Mother's Day card for a friend or a sister who is pregnant or who has just had a baby can be made with paper-casting techniques. Simply press paper pulp into a mold bearing the shape of a baby's foot, and then glue it onto the front of a card. A card front can also be made into a frame bearing a picture of your mother, grandmother, or a family grouping. Photo-frame cards are sure to join the family display atop the mantel.

FOLD THE PAPER IN THIRDS LENGTHWISE. In the center panel, use a pencil to trace around a 3-inch heart-shaped cookie cutter. Use an X-Acto knife and a cutting mat to neatly cut out the heart. Punch holes around the heart-shaped opening and weave narrow ribbon through them tabby style, tying it in a bow on the side of the card.

Use scissors to trim ⅛ inch off the bottom panel of the card and fold the panel away from you, toward the inside of the card, to see how it will be positioned behind the heart-shaped opening. Use dry adhesive to affix the photo to the inside of the folded panel so that the heart frames it. Glue the folded panel into position behind the opening.

Decorate the card by brushing white glue on the back of some pressed flowers and positioning them around the woven ribbon. *Note:* If you use a large-hole punch, enlarge the card enough so that the center panel will accommodate the larger weaving area. Use a smaller cookie cutter to create an opening to frame a smaller picture.

Handmade cards for
Mother's Day express
loving sentiments and
are beautiful keepsakes.

Cards for **Special Occasions**

You don't need a recognized holiday marked on the calendar to keep in touch with friends and family. If you consider your friends' interests, virtually any occasion can warrant a card. If you have friends who are avid baseball or football fans, you could send them a card celebrating the start of that sport's season. (Sympathy cards might also be sent to the wives who are not sports fans.)

In March, you might send northern-based gardening friends a card noting that it's time to plant the peas and wishing them a bountiful harvest. City dwellers might like to be reminded that spring is just around the corner with some pressed johnny jumps ups from your garden. The advent of spring is a joy to everyone and a card describing what is blooming and buzzing in your neck of the woods is always fun to read.

Summer might be a good time of year to send your sailing and biking friends a card wishing them a happy regatta season or good luck on the mountain bike trails. Crisp autumn afternoons and changing leaves in many parts of the country may inspire you to send a card celebrating the season with a bright red leaf decoration.

Pluck early spring pansies from the garden and press them in a heavy book. Then tuck them inside letters to herald the new season.

SUGGESTED ENCLOSURES

Confetti always makes a good enclosure for cards marking a celebration. Colorful metallic-tinted plastic confetti shaped like trees, cupids, shamrocks, and more is available in most card shops. Paper punches bearing a shape you wish to reproduce can also be used to create your own confetti.

Party decorations, such as the tiny American flags available for Fourth of July parties, can be sent along with your card to make the greeting more festive. Candy hearts or paper hearts cut from doilies can be enclosed in a card sent for Valentine's Day. You could send a packet of vegetable seeds or some pressed flowers to a gardening friend to celebrate the start of the growing season. Or you could enclose a packet of birdseed in a springtime card, noting your first robin sighting. Clover (especially a four-leaf clover) can be sent along with a Saint Patrick's Day card.

Like Emily Dickinson, you could make a tiny envelope to send living leaves and flowers. When she wrote to her intimate friend Susan, she enclosed some violets, saying, "They begged me to let them go . . . and with them as Instructor, a bit of knightly grass, who also begged the favor to accompany them — they are but small, Susie, and I fear not fragrant now, but they will speak to you of warm hearts at home."

Confetti, streamers, paper hearts, and tiny envelopes for pressed flowers are festive enclosures for special occasions.

RUBBER STAMPING

To make a rubber-stamped card, you'll need:

- Rubber stamp of a large snowflake
- Rubber-stamp pad with clear embossing ink
- Decorative and solid-color papers
- Embossing powder in your choice of color(s)
- Cotton swab or small brush
- Heat gun
- Scissors
- Decorative corner-rounding scissors
- Dry adhesive
- Prefolded card
- Foam tape

If you've never created a rubber-stamped card, you're in for a pleasant surprise. Rubber stamping is one of the easiest ways to create an image for a greeting card, and you can also combine or layer stamped images with decorative papers. You can create your own stamp by drawing or tracing a design on a large rubber eraser and using a V-shaped linoleum cutter and an X-Acto knife to cut away the parts of the design you don't want to print. Or use one of the millions of readymade stamps available in stores.

Try stamping the front of a folded card with colored inks using several related images. Or stamp a repeat design around the card's border and then glue an appropriate photo on top of the stamped designs.

Another option is to use one stamp to cover two different papers with stamped designs in different colors. Give each sheet a decorative edge, layer them, and then glue them to a card front. Create a gold embossed design and place it in the center. A Celtic knot is a good image to use for this design.

When choosing a stamp, think about the interests, hobbies, or upcoming events in the lives of your friends. If your friends are leaving soon for a ski vacation, you could send a card decorated with snowflakes. The card interior might read:

> *The cabin is warm and toasty, the jays are a splash of blue at the feeder, and the twin pines are so snow laden that they can barely hold up their branches.*
>
> *I can just picture you whizzing down Telluride mountain.*
>
> *Happy skiing.*

The interior of a card stamped with snowflakes might celebrate a friend's long-awaited ski vacation.

Rubber-stamped snowflakes are embossed, cut out, and attached to decorative paper with foam tape.

PRESS THE STAMP AGAINST THE CLEAR EMBOSSING PAD, then press the inked stamp firmly against the paper without rocking it. While the ink is still wet, sprinkle on the embossing powder. Tap the paper to spread the powder over the stamped image. Shake the excess powder onto a piece of folded paper so that it can easily be returned to the bottle. Use a cotton swab or a small brush to wipe away any powder that's clinging to parts of the paper you don't intend to emboss.

Heat the powder with the heat gun to melt it and create the embossed image. Cut out the embossed image with the scissors and set it aside. Use decorative corner-rounding scissors to cut ornate edges on a piece of decorative paper and another, slightly larger, piece of colored paper.

Attach the decorative paper to the top of the solid paper with dry adhesive and then onto the prefolded card. Affix the embossed image to the card front with foam tape, which will elevate it slightly from the background papers.

Artful Envelopes

Receiving a personal letter is practically cause for celebration these days, and the hand-addressed envelope is the first indication that what you've just found inside your mailbox is not a bill or a piece of junk mail.

Now that you've learned some easy, beautiful techniques for decorating cards and stationery, you can use them to **dress up your envelopes**, too.

Sir, more than kisses,

letters mingle souls;

For, thus

friends absent speak.

John Donne
to Sir Henry Wotton, circa 1598

Creative **Envelope** Ideas

Your letter will be even more treasured when it arrives in an envelope bedecked with leaves or with flowers tumbling from its borders. Even a few stamped snowflakes on the corner of an envelope show that you care enough about the recipient to make the envelope special.

You can add decorative accents to purchased envelopes or, if the card you have created doesn't fit into a standard-sized envelope, you can make one yourself. Large greeting cards often come with matching oversized envelopes, and you can easily steam them open and trace around them to make patterns for similarly sized handmade cards. You can also enlarge a pattern by using a ruler to measure an inch or so wider than the envelope's margins. Or you can purchase an envelope template from the wide variety available in craft stores. It's also fun to cut the envelope paper with edging scissors or to use an Art Deckle ruler to add more interest.

Addressing Envelopes

Playful letters should arrive in playfully addressed envelopes. When addressing a letter to a friend celebrating a special event, it's fun to alter the name of the recipient. Address your letter to The Birthday Girl, The New Mom, or The World Traveler. You can center the name and address, stagger them, or forget all that and let the creative muse guide you.

Try writing the address on a curve, making the letters bounce up and down or penning them in different colored inks. Lightly pencil in curved or straight lines to follow when composing the address and erase them later, or create the lines with gel pens and let them remain as part of the design. Your return address can be placed on the envelope flap, written in the upper-left-hand corner of the envelope, or integrated into the envelope's border decoration. As long as things are legible, your letter will arrive.

Try addressing envelopes in playful ways to create excitement about the contents.

Decorative Techniques

There are many techniques for decorating envelopes. Delicate border designs look sophisticated, but all-over designs in bright colors can be the perfect touch for casual correspondence. Don't be afraid to let your imagination run wild. You can always paste a plain piece of paper on top of a highly decorated envelope and write the address on that.

Leaf-Printed Designs

Leaf printing is a simple way to add color and pattern to an envelope. Tiny leaves look especially good as a border or all-over design. Because one leaf will often print an entire sheet of paper, you needn't gather many to do the job. I sometimes send catnip-printed envelopes to my cat-loving friends and enclose some dried leaves for their kitties.

Stenciling

A stenciled card with a matching stenciled envelope is really lovely. The stenciling can be a single accent, a border design, or a very pale, all-over pattern. A surprise image on the envelope flap is another possibility.

Rubber Stamping

Rubber stamps are perfect for decorating envelopes. You can choose a large snowflake stamp for heralding the ski season or a tiny rabbit stamp to make repeat designs around the edges of your envelope bearing an Easter card. Add dabs of textural fabric paint here and there to accentuate the design. The envelope can be even more dramatic if the stamping is thermal embossed with gold powder.

This leaf-printed envelope is perfect for a nature-loving friend.

Calligraphic Ornaments

Repeat marks made with chisel-edged pens or simple designs made with felt-tip markers can make interesting envelope decorations. Books on ornaments can provide you with appropriate designs to copy.

Embossing

To emboss an envelope, steam it open or gently separate the edges with a letter opener. After you've applied the design, reseal it with dry adhesive. Or add an embossed detail to the flap to coordinate with a similarly decorated card.

This unique envelope has four overlapping flaps that open from the center.

Coordinated Postage Stamps

The postage stamp that carries your letter across the miles is the jewel in the crown of your letter. Contrary to what you may think, many people do notice stamps. The wrong one can diminish your envelope design and leave your friend wondering if you have ever heard of commemorative stamps.

Go to the post office and ask to see a copy of *The U.S. Guide to Stamps*, which showcases the variety of stamps you can purchase. For example, there are stamps of athletes, artists, antique glass, 20th-century trains, and creatures of the rain forest and desert, to name just a few. Choose a stamp to coordinate with your envelope design, to highlight your friend's interests, or to suggest the content of your letter.

Gorgeous flowers and birds are perfect for summer correspondence, and Arctic wolves may be a nice theme for winter letters. Holiday stamps are also available, as are romantic Victorian stamps for love letters or Valentine's Day cards. Flags, of course, are a perennial favorite for Fourth of July notes.

However, some stamps aren't for everyone. The insect and wildlife stamps are colorful and exciting, but it's hard to believe that anyone other than an entomologist would like to see a picture of a spider on an envelope. Stamps bearing the pictures of snakes should also be reserved for nonphobic friends.

The post office carries a variety of commemorative stamps that are sure to suit just about any taste or interest.

Sealing Wax

Sealing wax has been used since the late 1600s to add a finishing touch to a letter. The wax seals the letter's contents and alerts the recipient if there has been a breach of privacy. Once reserved for letters between diplomats and lovers, sealing wax is again a popular stationery item. Many people have discovered the delight of dripping colorful wax onto an envelope flap and embossing a design in it with a brass stamp. You can find stamps bearing your initials, Celtic knots, flowers, astrological signs, and other images at stationery and gift shops.

How to Use Sealing Wax

1. Use a match to light the sealing wax wick and hold the dripping wax over the envelope's flap to deposit a thick layer.
2. While the wax is still wet, press a brass seal into it and hold it for a few seconds until the wax cools and creates an embossed design.

Colorful wax and a brass stamp seal an envelope with style.

Making Decorative Paper

Although there are lovely decorative papers available for purchase from artisans around the world, it's especially rewarding to make your own. Inexpensive papermaking kits can be purchased in craft stores and through art supply catalogs with instructions on how to use a blender to recycle unwanted mail into decorative paper. You can easily add flower petals, *bits of colored ribbon,* and other things to make your own unique stationery.

There is nothing to write about, you say. Well then, write and let me know just this — that there is nothing to write about; or tell me in the good old style if you are well.

Pliny the Younger

Specialty Techniques

Books such as *Paper Art*, *The Handmade Paper Book*, or *The Papermaker's Companion* (see Recommended Reading), will give you lots of ideas for how to turn a blank sheet of purchased or handmade paper into an artful piece of stationery. There are scores of techniques to try. Some are fairly complicated while others are quite simple.

Batik paper, for instance, will take some time. You'll need to repeatedly drip or paint hot wax onto a sheet of paper, coat the paper with successive color washes, then iron the wax out of the paper. On the other hand, sponge printing — dabbing paper with various paint-covered sponges — gives almost immediate results.

Two simple paper decorating techniques, *suminagashi* marbling and paste-paper design, can yield a stack of unique paper with just an afternoon's effort. Both techniques have been captivating artists for centuries. The papers can be used for letter writing and make striking collage and weaving materials for cards and envelopes. They also look sensational when layered with other papers on greeting cards or used as a background paper for a blank sheet of stationery. Both decorative techniques have been featured in a number of projects in this book. I hope the projects will inspire you to create your own beautiful stationery.

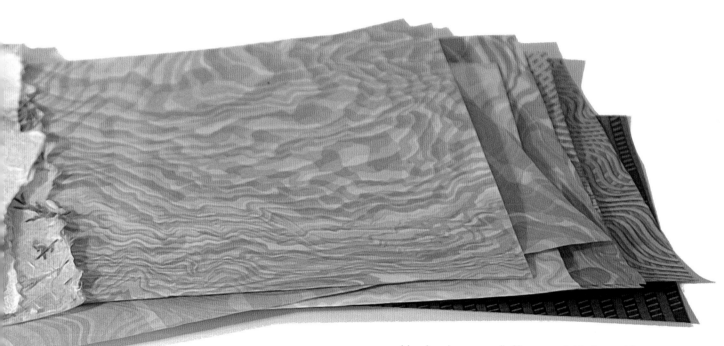

Handmade papers (left) are available in a wide range of colors, textures, and designs. *Suminagashi* marbling and paste-paper designs (right) are elegant decorative techniques.

SUMINAGASHI MARBLING

To make *suminagashi* paper, you'll need:

- Marbling tray (a plastic kitty-litter pan or a new photo tray can be used)
- Water
- Boku-Undo marbling colors
- Divided watercolor mixing tray that holds about one teaspoon of color
- Kodak Photo-Flo 200 in a small dropper bottle (or apply with an eyedropper)
- Three inexpensive bamboo brushes about 1¼ inches long with a tapered point
- Folding fan (optional)
- Oriental rice paper, hand-made paper, charcoal paper, or absorbent paper with a high cotton content
- Cookie sheet
- Drying rack or lines
- Heavy books or iron
- Newspaper cut into 2-inch-wide strips

Suminagashi, the oldest and simplest form of marbling, was practiced by members of Japan's royal court more than 800 years ago to make the background for early Japanese calligraphy. Both children and adults can make this beautiful paper by floating colored dyes on water, blowing on them to pattern them, and applying a piece of absorbent paper to make a one-of-a-kind print. If done in pale colors, you can use the paper as beautiful decorative stationery. Or you can paste a piece of plain stationery on top of *suminagashi* designs that are too dark to write on.

FILL A MARBLING TRAY, plastic kitty-litter pan, or new photo tray with two inches of water. Place a teaspoon each of two marbling colors in a divided watercolor mixing tray and add a single drop of Photo-Flo to each. This helps the colors float and spread. Place a teaspoon of water in another of the mixing tray's compartments and add a drop of Photo-Flo to the water to make a surfactant solution that will create clear rings.

Using a different brush for each color and for a clear solution, stir well. In the center of the water-filled tray, touch the surface of the water with a color-filled brush, releasing a circle of color. Dip the tip of another brush into the clear solution in the watercolor mixing tray. Touch the tip of the brush to the center of the ink in the water-filled tray, which will create a ring.

Alternate applying a color and then the clear solution until a number of concentric rings are formed. The more rings you create, the more complex your design will be. Fan or blow on the floating rings to create a design. Blow gently from the side of the tray to form meandering lines of color or blow sharply from above to form jagged lines. Waving a handheld fan over the tray will make the jagged lines even more pronounced.

Slowly lay a sheet of paper on top of the floating design. To do this, steady one hand at the far end of the tray and gradually roll the rest of the sheet down to avoid trapping an air bubble beneath the paper. The print is made as soon as the paper makes contact with the floating colors. Remove the paper by picking it up by the edges farthest from you. Place it on a cookie sheet, colored side up, for gentle rinsing if you see the colors bleeding. Hang it over a rack or a line to dry.

When the paper is dry, place it under some heavy books or iron it on the wrong side to flatten it. Drag a 2-inch-wide newspaper strip over the water's surface to remove excess color before marbling a second sheet.

As a variation, apply alternating color rings in several sections of the tray to create new designs. Instead of using just two colors, try marbling with several. Or hold two color brushes in one hand and the clear brush in the other to work more quickly. Try alternating color with clear solution or color with color to vary the open spaces in your design. Drag a single hair through the designs to gently pattern them.

You can also remarble a dry printed sheet to create a double-image "ghost print," as shown here. The intersecting lines and new colors formed when one color crosses another yields lovely paper. Try marbling typing paper and envelopes with a high cotton content in light colors to create beautiful matching stationery.

Marbling gives paper
a flowing, watery design.

- Cornstarch
- Water
- Measuring cup
- One-quart cooking pot
- Stirring spoon
- Fine strainer
- Several containers with lids (large enough to hold a 2- or 3-inch paintbrush)
- Teaspoon
- Heavy-body acrylic paint
- Sturdy nonabsorbent paper, such as drawing paper
- Pan of water
- Sheet of Plexiglas 2 inches larger all around than the paper you're decorating
- Sponge
- Two- or three-inch-wide housepainting brush
- Rubber paint-graining combs, plastic hair picks, or calligraphy pens
- Rubber stamps, chopsticks, plastic spackle knives, sponges, and crumpled newspaper (optional)
- Drying rack or lines
- Bucket of water
- Iron

PASTE PAPER

Paste-paper designs were once prized by 17th-century European bookbinders and originally used as book cover and endpapers. Paste paper is created by brushing colored paste onto a dampened sheet of paper, then making graphic patterns by displacing the paste with various tools. The process is simple, but the images can look very sophisticated. Most paste papers are too dark to write on except with light ink, but they can provide you with stunning designs for handmade cards and envelopes.

MAKE A STARCH PASTE by blending ¼ cup of cornstarch with ¼ cup of water. Add 1 more cup of water and heat on medium high while stirring, until it is almost boiling. (The paste will resemble thick custard.) Remove from the heat and stir in ½ cup of water. Cover and let the paste rethicken as it cools. The paste can be made the previous day or in the morning for use in the afternoon.

Strain the cooled paste into four separate containers. Stir about 3 teaspoons of acrylic color into each ½ cup of paste, depending on the intensity of color desired.

Relax the paper by wetting it briefly in a pan of water. Place the paper on a sheet of Plexiglas and use a sponge to stroke from the center outward, which presses out air bubbles and wrinkles and removes excess water. Use a 2- or 3-inch-wide housepainting brush to evenly coat the paper with a solid color paste or with stripes of different colors.

Use rubber graining combs, plastic hair picks, calligraphy pens, or other tools to create scalloped, wavy, or straight lines by drawing them across the paste-covered sheets. Try making marks in the paste with rubber stamps, chopsticks, plastic spackle knives, sponges, crumpled newspapers, and any other tools that might make interesting designs in the paste. Overlap patterns to create a three-dimensional effect.

When you've finished making designs in the paste, peel the paper off the Plexiglas and hang it over a rack or line to dry. After each paper is hung on the drying rack, wipe off the Plexiglas with the sponge dipped in the bucket of water. This removes the paste residue that will otherwise transfer to the back of the next sheet of paper and paste it down. Be sure to clean all your tools and brushes before the acrylic paint dries, which makes it hard to remove. When the paper is dry, iron it on the wrong side to flatten it.

As a variation, dampen a previously printed sheet of paper and coat it with another colored paste. Pattern this sheet to create a double-image design. The colors and patterns of the first image will show through the second, giving the paper added dimension. It's best to use plastic or rubber tools when making double-image designs, as the redampened paste can be fragile. You can also add PearlEx powder to the paint or use metallic acrylics and interference colors to make your papers sparkle.

You can make a variety of patterns with just one graining tool.

A Final Note

If you haven't been corresponding with handwritten letters lately, you'll be amazed at how quickly and enthusiastically your friends will respond to the extra attention you give them. A handwritten letter is truly an unusual gift these days and is all the more appreciated because it says "I care enough about you to steal time away from a busy day and spend it with you."

The intimate and often profound content of some handwritten letters will no doubt inspire you and your correspondents to save them to read again in the near or distant future. You can increase the likelihood of your letters lasting through the years by taking a few precautions. Use archival materials when creating your cards and letters, and encourage your letter-writing friends to do the same. Encase acidic enclosures, such as newspaper articles, in clear mylar envelopes to prevent them from ruining the letter itself.

To be on the safe side, always store your letters in the living area of your home where the temperature is moderate. It's charming to think of discovering old letters in a trunk in the attic, but attics can overheat and cause letters and accompanying photos to become stiff and brittle. Garages and basements tend to be damp, and letters stored there may become soggy and mildewed. Also, paper-munching insects may dine on your treasured letters stored in little-used spaces, and you may not discover their presence until it is too late. By preserving your letters, you will preserve your memories for yourself and perhaps for generations that follow.

Whether recounting the past or making promises for the future, the love that passes between correspondents is always felt between the lines. Writing letters encourages us to give voice to our thoughts and express the warmth that we feel for each other. By taking the time to silently correspond with a friend, you may reap the benefits of a calmer and more positive disposition. Like meditation or journal keeping, spending quiet, introspective moments at your writing desk or beneath an oak tree in your backyard will leave you feeling refreshed and connected to the important people in your life.

Recommended Reading

Bethmann, Laura Donnelly. *Nature Printing*. Pownal, VT: Storey Books, 2001.

Charatan, Karen. *ABC ZIG Calligraphy*. Clifton, NJ: EK Success, 1993.

Dorey, Sasha. *Decorative Stamping: Hundreds of Projects for Your Home*. Pownal, VT: Storey Books, 1995.

Dubay, Inga, and Barbara Getty. *Italic Letters: Calligraphy & Handwriting*. Portland, OR: Portland State University Continuing Education Press, 1992.

Hiebert, Helen. *The Papermaker's Companion: The Ultimate Guide to making and Using Handmade Paper*. Pownal, VT: Storey Books, 2000.

Hiebert, Helen. *Papermaking with Plants: Creative Recipes and Projects Using Herbs, Flowers, Grasses, and Leaves*. Pownal, VT, Storey Books, 1998.

James, Angela. *The Handmade Book*. Pownal, VT: Storey Books, 2000.

Maurer-Mathison, Diane. *The Ultimate Marbling Handbook*. New York, NY: Watson-Guptill Publications, 1999.

Maurer-Mathison, Diane, with Jennifer Philippoff. *Paper Art*. New York, NY: Watson-Guptill Publications,1997.

Ramsay, Angela. *The Handmade Paper Book*. Pownal, VT: Storey Books, 1999.

Saddington, Marianne. *Making Your Own Paper: An Introduction to Creative Papermaking*. Pownal, VT: Storey Books, 1992.

Supply Sources

Amsterdam Art
1013 University Avenue
Berkeley, CA 94710
(510) 649-4800
Art supplies, paper

Arnold Grummer's Paper-
   making Kits & Supplies
Greg Markim, Inc.
P.O. Box 13245
Milwaukee, WI 53213
(800) 453-1485
Papermaking kits, supplies

Carriage House Paper
P.O. Box 197
North Hatfield, MA 01066
(800) 669-8781
Papermaking supplies

Daniel Smith
P.O. Box 84268
Seattle, WA 98124
(800) 426-6740
www.danielsmith.com
Art supplies, papers

Diane Maurer Hand
   Marbled Papers
P.O. Box 78
Spring Mills, PA 16875
(814) 422-8651
*Boku-Undo marbling colors,
   decorative papers*

Dick Blick
P.O. Box 1267
Galesburg, IL 61402

(800) 447-8192
www.dickblick.com
Art supplies, papers

Dieu Donné Papermill
433 Broome Street
New York, NY 10013
(212) 226-0573
*Papermaking supplies,
   decorative papers*

Dreamweaver Stencils
1335 Cindee Lane
Colton, CA 92324
(909) 824-8343
*Stenciling and embossing
   supplies*

Fascinating Folds
P.O. Box 10070
Glendale, AZ 85318
(800) 582-2777
www.fascinating-folds.com
Papers, paper art supplies

Flax Art & Design
1699 Market Street
San Francisco, CA 94103
(415) 552-2355
www.flaxart.com
Papers, art supplies

Hollanders
407 North Fifth Avenue
Ann Arbor, MI 48104
(734) 741-7531
www.hollanders.com
Decorative papers

John Neal, Bookseller
1833 Spring Garden Street
Greensboro, NC 27403
(919) 272-7604
www.johnnealbooks.com
Calligraphy supplies

Kate's Paperie
561 Broadway
New York, NY 10012
(888) 941-9169
www.katespaperie.com
Art papers

La Papeterie St. Armand
950 Rue Ottawa
Montreal, Quebec
Canada H3C 1S4
(514) 874-4089
*Papermaking supplies,
   papers*

Lee S. McDonald, Inc.
523 Medford Street
P.O. Box 264
Charlestown, MA 02129
(617) 242-2505
Papermaking supplies

Nature's Pressed
P.O. Box 212
Orem, UT 84049
(800) 850-2499
www.naturespressed.com
Pressed leaves and flowers

Paper & Ink Books
P.O. Box 35
3 North Second Street
Woodsboro, MD 21798
(301) 898-7991
www.paperinkbooks.com
Calligraphy supplies

Paper Source, Inc.
232 West Chicago
Chicago, IL 60610
(312) 337-0798
Large selection of papers

Paper-Ya & Kakali
   Handmade Papers, Inc.
9-1666 Johnston Street
Granville Island, BC
Canada V6H 3S2
(604) 684-2531
Decorative papers

Pearl Paint Co. Inc.
308 Canal Street
New York, NY 10013
(800) 451-PEARL
www.pearlpaint.com
Art supplies, papers

Swallow Creek Papers
P.O. Box 152
Spring Mills, PA 16875
(814) 422-8651
Decorative papers

Index

NOTE: Page numbers in *italics* indicate photographs.

About the Author

DIANE MAURER-MATHISON is internationally recognized as an expert paper artist and is the author of *Fiber Arts, An Introduction to Carrageenan and Watercolor Marbling, Marbling, Decorative Paper, Art of the Scrapbook, Paper Art,* and *The Ultimate Marbling Handbook,* as well as *Make Your Own Spectacular Valentines,* a papercraft book for children. Diane specializes in marbling and paste-paper designs and has exhibited her work throughout the United States. Her decorative papers have been reproduced for stationery designs and greeting cards.

Diane's work is represented in the collections of the Cooper-Hewitt Museum of Decorative Arts and Design, the Institute for Book Arts, the Museum of New Mexico, the Nelson-Atkins Museum of Art, the Newberry Library, and the Pattee Library as well as the Dutch Royal Library in the Netherlands and the Suleymaniye Library in Turkey. Recent commissions of her work include designs for Godiva Chocolatier, Lenox China, and Harper Collins Publishers. She is included in the Who's Who reference book *2000 Outstanding Artists and Designers of the 20th Century* for her contributions to the paper arts.

An avid letter writer, Diane lives in Spring Mills, Pennsylvania, with her husband Jeffery, a graphic artist, and three cats and a dog, whose comical antics provide her with much to write about.